Reptiles

Edited by Belinda Gallagher
Cover design by Oxprint Ltd.

Published by Longmeadow Press, 201 High Ridge Road, Stamford,
CT 06904. All rights reserved. No part of this book may be
reproduced or utilized in any form or by any means,
electronic or mechanical, including photocopying, recording
or by any information storage and retrieval system, without
permission in writing from the Publisher.

Library of Congress Cataloging-in-Publication Data
ISBN: 0-681-45434-2
Printed in China
First Longmeadow Press Edition 1993
0 9 8 7 6 5 4 3 2 1

LEARN ABOUT

Reptiles

Written by Jane and David Glover
Illustrated by Brian Watson

LONGMEADOW
P R E S S

Millions of years ago, when the world was warmer, giant reptiles roamed the Earth. Dinosaurs lived on the land, ichthyosaurs and plesiosaurs swam in the seas, pterosaurs flew in the air. These giants have all disappeared, but there are still more than 6000 different kinds of reptile alive today.

Crocodiles, tortoises, lizards and snakes are all reptiles. They are cold-blooded. This means that in cold weather they cannot keep warm and active – so most of them live in hot places. Their thick, scaly skins stop them from drying out in the sun. They live in deserts and jungles, in rivers and in swamps. Some are meat-eaters, others are gentle plant-eaters.

Reptiles keep growing all their lives. The Galapagos giant tortoise lives for more than 100 years. Old ones are 4 feet (1.2 m) long and weigh twice as much as a man.

Tortoises move slowly but they can pull their heads and legs inside their shells for safety.

The African pancake tortoise has a soft shell. If it is attacked it squeezes between some rocks and puffs itself up until it is wedged tight.

All tortoises are plant-eaters. Spur-thighed tortoises eat grass and leaves. They live in warm countries in Europe and Africa. Thousands are collected and sold as pets. Many of them die when they are kept as pets in cold countries.

Snapping turtles are meat-eaters. They live in rivers and lakes. The snapper lies in wait amongst the weeds until a fish passes – then it shoots out its head and snaps its strong jaws shut.

Green turtles live in warm seas. Every two or three years the females swim to a deserted beach to lay their eggs. In the night they pull themselves up the beach and dig holes with their back flippers. They each lay about a hundred eggs, cover them with sand and return to the sea. Ten weeks later the eggs hatch. Thousands of baby turtles dig themselves out and rush down to the water. Many of them do not reach the sea. They are eaten by birds.

The female Nile crocodile is a good mother. She guards her nest by the water's edge. When the eggs hatch she takes her babies gently in her mouth and carries them to a safe spot. She looks after them until they can fend for themselves.

Nile crocodiles hunt silently. They lie in the water like old logs until a bird or a gazelle comes to the bank to drink – then they grab it and pull it into the water to drown.

The Indian gavial uses its long, thin snout to catch fish under water. It hardly ever comes onto land except to build its nest.

Crocodiles and alligators are the biggest, fiercest reptiles alive today. But many species are now quite rare. They have been hunted for their skins to make shoes and handbags. In some places, their swampland homes have been drained by farmers.

The biggest crocodiles live in rivers and swamps in Asia and Australia. They can be 20 feet (6 m) long.

The American alligator is nearly as big. It was in danger of extinction – but it is now protected from hunters and its numbers are increasing.

The spectacled caiman is a small South American crocodile. Its eyes are high on its head so that it can see above the water as it floats at the surface of the river.

There are more species of lizard than any other sort of reptile.

Most small lizards eat insects. In hot countries, geckos eat insect pests in houses. They can walk up walls or even upside-down on the ceiling using special pads on their feet. They are the noisiest lizards – the male makes a loud "gek-ho" sound to attract the female.

Some big lizards eat plants. Common iguanas eat leaves in jungle trees along river banks. They are good swimmers and can drop into the water if they are attacked.

The biggest lizard in the world is a meat eater. The komodo dragon can be 10 feet (3 m) long. It hunts wild pigs and deer.

The flying dragon is a small Asian tree lizard. It uses flaps of skin between its front and back legs as wings to glide from tree to tree.

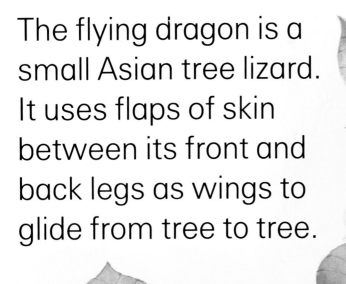

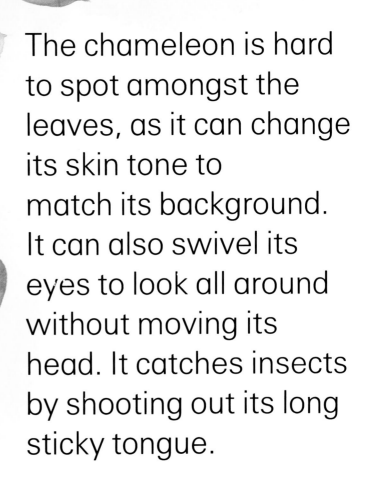

The chameleon is hard to spot amongst the leaves, as it can change its skin tone to match its background. It can also swivel its eyes to look all around without moving its head. It catches insects by shooting out its long sticky tongue.

The gila monster lives in deserts. It can go for months without eating – living on the fat in its thick tail. When it bites, poison runs down grooves in its teeth into its prey. Gila monsters are the only poisonous lizards – but they are not as poisonous as some snakes.

The Indian cobra uses its teeth like needles to inject poison into its prey. If it is attacked, it can spit poison 6 feet (2 m) into its enemy's eyes.

The coral snake's bright skin warns that it is dangerous and should be left alone.

Adders are the only poisonous snakes in Britain. When the sun shines they bask on hillsides to warm up. If they hear something coming they move away – they are only dangerous if they are attacked or stepped on by accident.

The rattle snake shakes its tail to warn that it is nearby. The rattle is made from pieces of hard skin left behind when the rattler sheds its skin as it grows.

The Indian python is one of the largest snakes in the world. It hunts at night. It has special pads near its nostrils to detect the heat given out by rats and small deer. It is not poisonous but coils around its prey and squeezes it until it suffocates.

The female python lays 100 eggs in a hole or a tree hollow. She coils around them and incubates them for about 10 weeks.

The South American anaconda is even longer than the python. It can grow to 9 m (30 ft). The female does not lay her eggs but keeps them inside her body until they hatch, then she gives birth to as many as 40 live young.

Reptiles quiz

Now you have read about reptiles how many of these questions can you answer? Look back in the book for help if you need to.

True or false?
1. All reptiles are meat-eaters.
2. Some reptiles live for a hundred years.
3. Crocodiles care for their young.
4. Lizards are all poisonous.
5. Lizards cannot swim.
6. Pythons are poisonous.

Odd one out.
Which is the odd one out and why?

7. Gila monster Gecko Gavial

8.   Chameleon   Anaconda   Iguana

9.   Caiman   Python   Tortoise

Answers

1. False – tortoises and some lizards eat plants.
2. True – the Galapagos giant tortoise does.
3. True.
4. False – Gila monsters are the **only** poisonous lizards.
5. False – some can – the iguana is a good swimmer.
6. False – it kills its prey by squeezing it.
7. Gavial – it's a crocodile, the other two are lizards.
8. Anaconda – it's a snake, the other two are lizards.
9. Tortoise – it's a plant eater, the others are meat eaters.